The Palm
of my
Heart

Poetry by African American Children

edited by **DAVIDA ADEDJOUMA**

illustrated by **GREGORY CHRISTIE**

introduction by **LUCILLE CLIFTON**

LEE & LOW BOOKS INC. NEW YORK

With much love and affection to my father,
David Kilgore, for filling my childhood with visual poetry,
my son, Charles Kilgore, for the poet he is, and my
grandson, La'Dra Hodges Kilgore, for the poet he is becoming
—D. A.

To my mother, Mrs. Ludria St. Amant-Christie, and to
my father, Mr. Gerard Christie, your support
continues to move these hands, while at the same time your
love continues to move this heart. I love you both
—G. C.

LEE & LOW BOOKS, Inc., 95 Madison Avenue, New York, NY 10016

Printed in Hong Kong by South China Printing Co. (1988) Ltd.

Art Direction and Design by Lou DiLorenzo
Book Production by Our House
The text is set in Gill Sans, Rockwell, and Sabon
The illustrations are rendered in acrylic and colored pencil

10 9 8 7 6 5 4 3 2
First Edition

Library of Congress Cataloging-in-Publication Data
The palm of my heart/edited by Davida Adedjouma;
illustrated by Gregory Christie—1st ed.
p. cm.
Summary: A collection of poems written by Afro-American children celebrating
what it means to be Black.
ISBN: 1-880000-41-5
1. Afro-American children's writings. 2. Children's poetry, American. 3. Afro-
Americans—Juvenile poetry. [1. Afro-American children's writings. 2. American
poetry—Afro-American authors—Collections. 3. Afro-Americans—Poetry.
4. Children's writings.]
I. Adedjouma, Davida. II. Christie, Gregory, ill.
PS591.N4P25 1996
811'.540809282'08996073—dc20   96-13426
CIP
AC

EDITOR'S NOTE

It has been my pleasure to conduct a series of writing workshops with children from the Inner City Youth League and the African-American Academy for Accelerated Learning (AAAL). These **Writing Between the Lines** workshops were designed to share my love of language, introduce children to the techniques of image and metaphor, narrative and dialogue, and then set them free to explore their own lives, feelings and imaginations.

My interest in teaching stems from the belief that the gift of culture must be passed from generation to generation. From first through eighth grade, I enjoyed the privilege of being educated in an all-black school on Chicago's South Side. I will be forever grateful to Gwendolyn Brooks, for the time she took to visit our classes and for instilling in me a love of poetry, to Charlemaine Rollins, for her marvelous storytelling, and to Mildred Johnson, for demonstrating the power of performed text. Each taught me that art was not just a luxury for the very few, but a tool of survival for many. Each taught me that creativity could and **should** be applied equally to math and science, English and Social Studies. Without this early exposure, I would not have become a writer.

Achievement is not reached individually, but through collective force. I wish to thank Sister Shirley Alexander and Brother Kwame McDonald of the Inner City Youth League, and Mother Katie Sample of AAAL for introducing me to the wonderful writers you are about to read. I want to thank the parents of these writers for having the vision to enroll their children in after-school and summer enrichments programs. And thank you, Liz Szabla, for seeing the power in a small chapbook, and wanting it to reach a larger audience.

I hope this anthology will challenge other African American youth to explore creativity as a means of self-definition. Because they who control the image, control the idea. And they who control the idea, control the mind.

—Davida Adedjouma

INTRODUCTION

When I was a girl, back in the dim late thirties and forties, the word "Black" was fighting language. None of us would have described ourselves in what we considered so negative a way. In fact, in a way that the world around us seemed to consider negative, for what was evil and ugly and unwanted in word or deed but darkness, but Black?

How wonderful to have come through that to this; to this treasure of young people and the treasury of their words. Here dark is equated with wonderful and Black with joy! "Lovely," the young poet says, "as the palm of my heart." Lovely, indeed. And aren't we lovely in our variety? And lucky too!

— *Lucille Clifton*

Black stride? It's:

the arch of my back

the curve of my spine

the way I stand

and my stance

is

pride.

PRE'CHEZZ RUDOLPH

Black culture is a secret

shared in the night.

A whispered thought,

the wonders of the mind,

a swirling of belief.

T. J. MOORE, JR.

Black is the color of some people

but people are different

differences are good because

no one else says the

same things as you.

SHAWNTA'YA JONES

Black is as dark as me

& my name is

Tyler.

TYLER MATTHEW ARMOUR

Black is a color

the color of me

& I ...

is me.

BRITTNEY JACKSON-TAYLOR

Black hands

are beautiful. They wiggle,

wwwhhh,

like the wind.

RATISHA HAWKINS

Black is brown

brown is the color of my skin

my skin is beautiful

and I am a **child**

of God.

RAYKEISHA JONES

Black is beautiful

as beautiful as white people

beautiful

as April.

SHELTONN LA'MAR JOHNSON

Black is pretty,

pretty is cute, and

I'm cute ...

when I **smile.**

RASHONDA HAWKINS

Black is dark,

dark is lovely,

lovely is **the palm of my heart**

and my heartbeats are filled with joy.

FELICIA RENEE BRAZIL

Black poetry

is a dance in the sand,

a song from a faraway land.

Come, let's dance and sing a song,

all night long.

ERICA NICOLE ROSE

Black imagination:

letters printed in a book

sitting there

waiting to be read.

TONISHA ANNETTE FARMER

Black is a heart

the heart is an African symbol of life

and life is good

life is good.

AARON MATTHEW FLOMO

Black power is freedom,

the strength to live

life

long.

MYISHA PATRICE FARMER

Black ancestors
died for my **freedom.**

My great uncle Jimmy risked
his life to help
Black people vote.

My great great grandmother voted
for the first time
when she was
80 years old.

Black **is boldness.**

BRANDON N. JOHNSON

Black history flows

through our veins

like **blood.**

SHANNON CHAVERS

Black ancestors

are you, my brother

and me.

BRIANA E. JOHNSON

Black is:

my parents thanking God for our food

my father — working to make a way for our

family

my mother — as strong as she can be

my brother — trying to wash dishes

and me — talking too much, me hitting

my cousin (not meaning to, really),

me playing basketball and

calling all the shots.

THELMA LOUISE LEE

Black is beautiful

Black is me

Black is *the* color

    can't you see

    that

blue **is** nice,

and orange is neat

But they can't compete

    because

Black is beautiful

Black is me

Tall, dark, and wonderful

    see!

ANDREYA RENEE ALLEN

Black spirit turns and churns

it **is** energetic and **eternal.**

LAUREN CRISLER

About the Poets

Andreya Renee Allen *was born in 1984. When she grows up, Andreya would like to be a singer, part-time writer, and the first black president of the United States. Andreya dedicates this poem to her family.*

Tyler Matthew Armour *was born in 1988 and enjoys rollerblading, Lego building, reading and watching cartoons. When Tyler grows up, he would like to be either a firefighter or a police officer.*

Felicia Renee Brazil *was born in 1985. When she's not writing, Felicia plays with her extensive Barbie doll collection. She would like to be a gymnast and writer.*

Shannon Chavers *was born in 1984 and studies jazz and tap dancing. When she grows up, Shannon would like to become a lawyer who specializes in the issues surrounding Oceanography Science.*

Lauren Crisler *was born in 1983. When she's not reading, Lauren sews, cooks and bakes, and earns money babysitting. Lauren's goal is to become a history professor.*

Myisha Patrice Farmer *was born in 1982 and enjoys bike riding and taking long walks with her friends. Myisha plans to become a veterinarian.*

Tonisha Annette Farmer *was born in 1984. She enjoys bike riding and rollerblading. When she grows up, Tonisha wants to teach kindergarten.*

Aaron Matthew Flomo *was born in 1988. His hobbies include writing stories and acting, swimming, and playing t-ball and tennis. Aaron's future plans are to be a movie producer and actor.*

Rashonda Hawkins *was born in 1985. She enjoys painting and modeling. Rashonda's goals include winning an Olympic medal in track.*

Ratisha Hawkins *was born in 1987. When she grows up, Ratisha wants to be a singer.*

Brittney Shadé Jackson-Taylor *was born in 1987. Brittney enjoys math and would like to teach second grade when she grows up.*

Brandon N. Johnson *was born in 1986 and enjoys playing hockey and creating worlds with Legos and K'nex. When Brandon grows up, he would like to be a scientist and play professional hockey.*

Briana E. Johnson *was born in 1988. She enjoys swimming and arts and crafts. When Briana grows up she wants to be a teacher during the day and a doctor at night.*

Sheltonn La'Mar Johnson *was born in 1987. His hobbies include rollerblading, football, computers, and reading and writing poetry. When he grows up, Sheltonn would like to be a firefighter.*

Raykeisha Jones *was born in 1984. Raykeisha loves to write, and would like to be a ballerina and an actress.*

Shawnta'ya Jones *was born in 1987. Her hobbies include dancing and cooking.*

Thelma Louise Lee *was born in 1984. Her hobbies are writing, dancing, talking, sewing, and reading.*

Thomas (T.J.) Moore, Jr. *was born in 1984. When he's not acting or writing, he plays a mean game of basketball. T.J. plans to become an actor and writer.*

Erica Nicole Rose *likes singing and dancing.*

Pre'Chezz Rudolph *was born in 1984. Pre'Chezz enjoys dancing and talking on the phone, and earns money babysitting in her free time.*